THE MAGIC
TOUCH

Also by Gila Manolson

Outside/Inside: A Fresh Look at Tzniut

Head to Heart: What to Know Before Dating and Marriage

THE MAGIC TOUCH

A Jewish Approach to Relationships

by Gila Manolson

TARGUM/FELDHEIM

First edition published 1992
Revised and expanded edition published 1999, 2005

Copyright © 1999, 2005 by Gila Manolson
ISBN 1-56871-185-9

Published by:
TARGUM PRESS, INC.
22700 W. Eleven Mile Rd.
Southfield, MI 48034
E-mail: targum@netvision.net.il
Fax: 888-298-9992
www.targum.com

Distributed by:
FELDHEIM PUBLISHERS
208 Airport Executive Park
Nanuet, NY 10954

Printing plates by Frank, Jerusalem
Printed in Israel by Chish

To my incredible husband,

Avraham,

*without whose support
this book would never
have been written.*

RABBI ZEV LEFF
Rabbi of Moshav Matityahu
Rosh Hayeshiva Yeshiva Gedola Matisyahu

הרב זאב לף
מרא דאתרא מושב מתתיהו
ראש הישיבה ישיבה גדולה מתתיהו

d.n. modiin 71917 ד.נ. מודיעין   tel. 08-976-1138 טל׳   fax 08-976-5326 פקס

I have had the pleasure of reading *The Magic Touch: A Jewish Approach to Relationships,* by Gila Manolson. Mrs. Manolson is a very talented, Torah-observant, God-fearing woman, and the wife of a Torah scholar. Recognizing the need, she has made an impressive and praiseworthy attempt to address a problem that affects a significant number of young adults from religious homes.

Ideally, a true Torah approach to male-female interaction — founded on a healthy degree of separation of the sexes — should characterize Jewish life, rendering this book and its arguments unnecessary. Unfortunately, many teenagers and young adults from observant homes face a challenge of enormous proportion. The society that surrounds and inevitably influences them idealizes casual relations between the sexes, and scorns individuals who conduct themselves otherwise. A religious upbringing is at times incapable of counteracting these influences, and the schools available in many communities are often limited in their ability to instill appreciation of the eternal validity of Torah and its way of life.

בס״ד

Moshav Shitufi   **מושב שיתופי**
d.n. modiin   71917   ד.נ. מודיעין
tel.   08-976-1016   טל׳
fax   08-976-1124   פקס

As a result, many young people compromise the Torah's ideals in favor of a lifestyle that appears more attractive. Others manage to observe the Halachah but without great conviction, constantly beset with doubts generated by peer pressure. Both these significant segments of the religious community need fortification if they are to uphold the values of the Torah and transmit them to their own children.

Based on a Talmudic discussion of certain popular practices that were at odds with Halachah (*Sotah* 48a), Rav Moshe Feinstein, *zt"l*, derives the following guiding principle: Where a situation contravenes Halachah but one cannot right it entirely, he is bound to at least improve it (*Igrot Moshe*, vol. 1, *Yoreh Deah* 53).

So, too, in the realm of male-female relationships, even if we may not be able to reverse the current trend, we must at least strive for greater conformity to Halachah.

The Torah's directives are ultimately unfathomable to the human intellect. We observe them simply because God has so commanded. However, God made these precepts somewhat comprehensible to us in order to enhance our observance. Furthermore, Rambam distinguishes between suprarational laws, such as kashrut, and those whose value is instinctively understood. Within this latter category are the laws of sexual morality. The generation of the flood was punished for its promiscuity even though these laws had not yet been revealed, for reason alone was expected to be humanity's guide. Therefore, even when based on purely rational grounds, sexually moral behavior is to be encouraged.

Hence, this book will serve both those who are already observant, who will appreciate the author's perspective on the benefits of sexual morality, and those who will accept God's commands only after being convinced of their wisdom and beauty.

In light of this readership, *The Magic Touch* makes a valuable contribution to the Jewish community. While by no means exhausting all the reasons for being *shomer negiah*, this work argues an intelligent and persuasive case on practical grounds, and in language its audience will relate to.

I found The *Magic Touch* informative and inspiring and am confident that, by virtue of the pure and noble intentions of its author, it will strengthen Torah observance in this crucial area.

With Torah blessings,

Rabbi Zev Leff

CONTENTS

Preface

While *The Magic Touch* has been written from a Torah perspective, it also reflects my own feelings and insights stemming from many years in *kiruv* (Jewish outreach). Because the presentation is therefore very personal, I'd first like to tell you a little about myself, and why I wrote this book.

I am a Jewish woman who grew up in a largely assimilated home in the northeastern United States. After graduating college and working for a year, I got the itch to travel and took off for Europe. I ended up in Israel, where I soon encountered Judaism. In my day, there were no classes for people off the street demonstrating the historical accuracy of Biblical prophecies or the codes hidden in the Torah and revealed by computer research. My interest in Judaism was sparked solely by what I sensed to be its wisdom regarding how to live a meaningful life. And as I consider human relationships to be at the center of our existence, as do most people, it was largely Judaism's approach to this powerful part of life that moved me to explore Torah. Little by little, other pieces of the puzzle came together, and eventually I embraced Torah in full.

In a way, this book began writing itself on my first Tishah B'Av (the day of mourning commemorating the destruction of the First and Second Temples). It was around two o'clock in the morning, and I was sitting on the roof of an old building overlooking the Kotel (Western Wall). I had recently learned that anyone who mourns the destruction of the Temple will rejoice in its rebuilding. That sounded like a pretty good deal to me. So I gazed at the Temple Mount, trying to grasp the loss of the Temple and experience true grief, maybe even enough to shed some tears. Pondering the priestly services that were no more — and about which I understood little — didn't do it, and being a vegetarian, I wasn't sure how mournful I felt over being unable to offer animal sacrifices. So instead, I tried focusing on the sorry decline we've experienced in human interaction.

Almost immediately, my mind moved to male-female relationships. The more I dwelled on it, the more I was struck by the utter lack of clarity that pervaded society, the illusions with which so many people entered into relationships, and the pain that resulted when things inevitably didn't work out. I felt grateful for having been spared so much of what others suffered. At the same time, I thought about the many good, sincere, and sensitive people I knew, people who were seeking something real, meaningful, and lasting and yet, as victims of the times, were experiencing failure and unhappiness. Even those not hurting outright were suffering subtle and irreparable damage to their sensitivity and trust. And it was all so needless. Suddenly I was overwhelmed by this vast human loss, and I cried.

Many years have passed since then. I'm still in Jerusalem, happily married to a wonderful man. I've worked extensively in *kiruv*, and my husband and I have hosted innumerable Shabbat (Sabbath) guests. In every context, I've found that relationships are among the foremost issues on people's minds.

A few years ago, encouraged by my husband and by my own love of talking, I started teaching about relationships as part of the now well-known Discovery program. Back then, Discovery was offered only to non-observant tourists; however, it often happened that uninspired religious high school graduates switched their *kippot* (yarmulkes) to baseball caps, or hitched up their skirts and sleeves, and sneaked in. Consequently, I usually faced people from a wide variety of backgrounds and lifestyles. One of the main ideas I discussed was being *shomer negiah*, abstaining from physical contact with the opposite sex before marriage. This was something radical and unheard of among the secular crowd and a familiar but controversial topic among those from religious homes. Yet almost everyone had the same response: "Hmm. This really makes sense. I've never heard things explained this way before." Which led me to question: "How come religious high school graduates have never heard this approach? And if it makes so much sense, shouldn't more people know about it?"

So it was that, soon afterwards, I came home from one of my classes and announced to my husband, Avraham, that I was going to write a book about being *shomer negiah*. Knowing that I had never authored so much as an article for the local newspaper, Avraham greeted my declaration with a quizzical smile that clearly said, "Are you serious?" I informed him that I was and, to prove it, asked if he had any ideas for the title. He continued looking at me. I repeated my request. Finally he realized I meant it. I waited in anticipation of a brilliant title that would sell a million copies.

Avraham tilted back in his chair. "How about *Hands Off, Buddy*?"

Very funny. "No, no, no," I replied tolerantly. "That's so negative. I want something positive, glowing, inspirational..."

He grinned. "I've got it. How about *The Beauty of Saying 'Hands Off, Buddy'*?"

The title could wait. Meanwhile, I started writing. And after much labor, the book was born, bearing Avraham's final title suggestion: *The Magic Touch: A Candid Look at the Jewish Approach to Relationships*.

To my immense delight, *The Magic Touch* outsold all expectations, and some schools even made it part of their curriculum. It was translated into French, and a pocket-sized Hebrew edition was widely distributed in Israel. Apparently, it filled a need.

In the meantime, as I continued teaching, I was asked more questions that I felt the book should address. The additional material I consequently gathered, coupled with the success of the original book, convinced me to publish this revised, expanded edition, which includes more ideas and true stories illustrating the power of a great Jewish idea.

In this new version of *The Magic Touch,* I'd like to share with you even more of the thoughts I've shared with participants in Discovery and numerous other programs since — many of which, while not all so sad, go back to what I was thinking, way back when, on that rooftop overlooking the Kotel.

G.M.
Jerusalem

Acknowledgments

Hashem, the source of all blessing, has made many special people part of my life, and (whether aware of it or not) they've all have contributed to this book. I want to express my heartfelt appreciation to at least some of them:

To my parents, for instilling in me the self-confidence that has fueled all my endeavors;

To Bracha Zaret, for opening the door to everything that has followed;

To Tziporah Heller, my teacher, mentor, and friend, for sharing with me what is surely but a fraction of her knowledge, wisdom, and insight;

To the wonderful educators at Neve Yerushalayim, among them Rabbi Dovid Refson and Rabbi Dovid Gottlieb, as well as to Rabbi Nathan Lopes Cardozo, for enriching my life immeasurably; and with special gratitude to Rabbi Shraga Silverstein, whose book *The Antidote: Human Sexuality in a Torah Perspective* has impacted profoundly on my awareness;

To the people who have given me such rich opportunities to grow in *kiruv* and teaching: Rabbi Meir Schuster, director of Heritage House; the directors of Aish HaTorah's Discovery seminar and the

Jerusalem Fellowships; Rabbi Reuven Grodner and Shalom Dinerstein, directors of the Beit Midrash Program of the Hebrew University of Jerusalem; Rabbi David Aaron, director of the Isralight Institute; and (thanks to Toby Kramen) Rabbi Chaim Pollock, director of the overseas program at Michlalah Jerusalem College for Women;

To Rabbi Yaakov Levy and Rabbi Dovid Orlofsky, from whose lectures this book and I have both benefited; and to Chana Appel and Liz Kaufman, for sharing with me their own stories from Discovery;

To my unique and wonderful friends: Tova Saul, Shaina Buchwald, Sarah Wurtzel, and Dena Estrin, who have taught, helped, and supported me in more ways than they realize; Debbie Kirschner, for her astute comments; and Batya Friedman, whose insightful mind and wise heart have blessed not only my writing but my life;

To my students, for challenging me and helping me develop my ideas;

To Rabbi Yaakov Rapoport, for his encouragement and his vital role in getting the original edition into print;

To my children, Chananya Baruch, Elyashiv Devir, Yair Simcha, Temima Sara, Emuna Rachel, Ayelet Ora, and Yisrael Leib, for putting up with my preoccupation at the computer;

And finally, to my loving husband, Avraham, for his invaluable critiquing of the manuscript (and for coming up with the perfect title). Beyond that, no words — not even another book in itself — could possibly do justice to all that he has done and continues to do for me.

Introduction

This is a book about touching — in Hebrew, *negiah*. Touch is undeniably one of the most pleasurable things in life. It can also be one of the most problematic. For touch, as casually as it's regarded in many circles, is far more powerful than most of us appreciate.

Judaism, always an astute observer of the human scene, believes that men and women who are not close relatives should be extremely reserved about expressing affection for one another through touch. In short, Judaism says: unless you're married to each other, don't. Understandably, this strikes some people as extreme. Consequently, while being *shomer negiah* is no less obligatory than observing Shabbat or *kashrut* (the dietary laws), some consider it a greater challenge. But for anyone who's serious about getting the most out of a relationship, being *shomer negiah* makes eminent sense.

This book explains why.

(Note: While I have changed people's names to protect their privacy, the stories included herein are true.)

CHAPTER ONE

The Superglue of Human Relations

I magine yourself in the following situation: You and a stranger are having a heated argument. Tempers are rising, and with them the decibel level, until you are practically shouting at each other. Realizing things are getting out of hand, your opponent interjects, "Hold on — let's try and calm down." It doesn't work. You are still furious. He or she then leans forward, puts a hand on your arm, and says, "Wait a minute." Suddenly, for some reason, you feel powerless to continue screaming. Your anger abates and you concede, perhaps even resentfully, to the suggestion.

Now imagine yourself at a checkout counter. You always dread entering this store because it takes so long to get out. Today is no exception — you have been waiting for what seems like an eternity to pay for your purchase. Finally your turn comes. You hand the slow-moving cashier your money. Usually you have to pick up your change off the counter, but today the cashier places it in your hand, and for a brief moment you feel the warmth of his or her hand on yours. Outside afterwards, you sense something strange. For some reason, you're feeling more warmly toward this store than before.

One more scene: You have just finished dining at a restaurant. The service has been exceedingly slow. Your waiter, Dave, finally brings the bill. "Hope you enjoyed your meal," he says with a smile and a parting pat on the shoulder. Watching him return to the kitchen, you suddenly feel a surge of generosity and leave a far bigger tip than you had intended. On your way out, you comment to the manager about how little waiters earn for working so hard. "It all depends," he replies. "Take this new guy, Dave. We don't know how he does it, but he pulls in at least thirty percent more in tips than anyone else."

In each of the above incidents (all based on true stories), you have fallen prey to one of the most subtle yet powerful forces in human relations: Touch.

Notice, incidentally, that not once was the contact sensual or even affectionate. Still, touch had an undeniable effect. It awakened within you warmth and receptivity, conscious or unconscious, toward the other person. Even when devoid of desire, touch left you feeling distinctly closer and more connected.

Touch could be called the Superglue of human relations. Take two clean surfaces, and Superglue will immediately stick them together. Touch between people works the same way. Take two people unopposed to feeling closer to one another, and touch between them will do the trick: Presto, they'll feel closer.

If even a simple touch can make this kind of

impact, imagine when it's coupled with a healthy dose of physical attraction. A ripple of warm feelings can become an emotional tidal wave.

Make yet another leap of imagination: You are eating at a cafeteria table with several other people. Among them, sitting quite close to you, is a person of the opposite sex to whom you have long felt attracted. Because you have seen no indication that he or she feels anything similar towards you, you have held back your feelings, silently suffering the agony of unrequited passion. Then, without warning, he or she turns in your direction, smiles, reaches for the salt, and happens to touch your hand. Were you to be instantly transformed into Barbra Streisand, you might actually be inspired to burst into ecstatic song, celebrating the tingle, the sparkle, the glow created by that touch (which you are convinced couldn't have been accidental); rhapsodizing about how the world has become so alive and shining; and finally crescendoing to a dramatic climax in which you proclaim: "SUDDENLY, NOTHING IS THE SAME!!!"

Yes, maybe I'm exaggerating. And so, perhaps, was Streisand, when she recorded "He Touched Me," the very song described above. But "He Touched Me" appears on an album of her greatest hits, so everyone apparently knew what she was singing about.

Now return to yourself, and imagine your reaction if this person to whom you're attracted were to give you something even more enjoyable than just a casual touch. Barbra Streisand, move over!

Why is such a simple, pleasurable experience misinterpreted as something more in many people's minds (particularly women's, as we'll see later)?

If you want something badly enough, you can fool yourself into believing you have it, even when what you have is only superficially similar. God created us to feel, when we're single, the ache of incompleteness. Consequently, one of our strongest desires is to experience the wholeness that comes from being genuinely close to another person. Because you want to *be* close, and physical contact makes you *feel* close, you are liable to believe that you *are* close — while, in fact, feeling close and being close are quite different. Touch can blur your perception of reality to the point where you mistake skin-to-skin contact for a heart-to-heart connection, leaving you with delusions of intimacy where no true intimacy exists.

Anything this powerful has to be handled carefully. Superglue can join two pieces of a broken plate — or two of your fingers. Similarly, touch — and particularly the "more than casual" kind — will make you feel closer to someone, irrespective of who he or she is and whether a real bond is ever likely to develop between you.

If touch were commercially produced and packaged, the following would be printed on the tube in bold red: "WARNING: USE WITH EXTREME CAUTION. Bonds instantly and indiscriminately."

The instructions would be equally unequivocal: "Use only after marriage. Touch will then express and cement your genuine connection. If used any earlier, touch will generate feelings of closeness with no basis in reality."

And that is playing with fire.

CHAPTER TWO

"Now You See It —
Now You Don't"

Touch creates a bond. If you're smart, before bonding with another person, you'll make sure that bond reflects something genuine and is therefore one you really want. To gain that clarity, you really have to know who he or she is. That requires objectivity. Unfortunately, objectivity comes about as naturally to most humans as bicycling does to a hippopotamus.

Imagine yourself at a party, chatting with two members of the opposite sex. One you find extremely attractive, the other not. You say something — and they respond identically. Whose response sounds better?

If the mere sight of a good-looking person sends your objectivity out for a coffee break, once you start touching, it steps out for lunch. From that moment on, you see what you want to see — and not the rest.

An incident from some years ago has stuck with me because of what it reveals about the delusions physical closeness can create. After college, I considered applying to graduate school in clinical psychology. My uncle, a psychotherapist, invited me to gain a firsthand glimpse of the profession by participating in a group therapy session he was leading. Much of that evening focused on a woman of about 25 as she poured out her painfully conflicted feelings about her boyfriend.

"Sometimes he treats me great, and sometimes he treats me like dirt," she explained through her tears. "I know I love him, but half the time I feel such anger towards him. One day I think we have such a wonderful thing going, and the next day I want to break up and never see him again."

Clearly, this guy was not so lovable and the relationship not so wonderful, but no one had the courage to tell her. Finally my uncle spoke up.

"This guy is poison for you," he told her straight out. "Can't you see that?"

Taken aback by his forcefulness, she immediately reacted: "But sometimes it feels so good, so right being with him."

"Listen to everything you've said," my uncle persisted. "This is not what I would call a good guy or a healthy relationship."

She looked at him uncomprehendingly. "But I feel so close and connected to him."

In short, she couldn't hear the truth.

People become enmeshed in "unhealthy" relationships for countless reasons. But a big complicating factor in nearly every case is the introduction of physical involvement quite early on. As soon as such closeness occurs on any level, that all-too-familiar rose-colored cloud descends, enveloping everything in the warm glow of intimacy. Once this bonding takes place, you can kiss much of your perspective good-bye. By the time this woman had detected serious flaws in her boyfriend, their physical connection had left her so emotionally attached to him that she could no longer step back and see reality.

During a Discovery seminar, when I was discussing the idea of maintaining objectivity by keeping one's distance, one of the participants raised her hand.

"You know," she told me, "a recent article in *Cosmopolitan* said the same thing. It was called 'How to Find Mr. Right,' and it recommended that if you want as much clarity as possible about a guy, you shouldn't get heavily physically involved for the first *thirty* dates."

How about that? I thought. A secular magazine had picked up on some practical Jewish wisdom applicable far beyond the Jewish world. Could *Cosmo* actually be heralding a return to sexual conservatism? I smiled to myself. Now, if Discovery and *Cosmo* ever joined forces, the possibilities would be endless....

CHAPTER THREE

The Strongest Love Potion

We have seen how touch can create illusions of closeness that blur your objectivity regarding your partner and your relationship with him or her. Refraining from physical contact does just the opposite. It creates the space for something real to develop and for you to appreciate that realness. And one way is by pushing a major kind of game-playing out of the picture.

When two people know that getting physical is part of the script for their relationship, a large placard appears in the wings, bearing, for all to read, the Schedule of Expected Increasing Physical Closeness. (Actually, I prefer to call it the G.A.M.E. — Generally Assumed Mating Expectations.)

You're probably grinning, knowing full well what I mean. In case you don't, let me explain. In every typical male-female relationship, it's understood that the physical side is going to progress according to a certain Schedule, given the norms within your particular social circle. If you're exceptionally wholesome and old-fashioned, the Schedule may proceed very slowly and never pass a certain point before marriage. At the other extreme, sometimes an impressive amount of activity is compressed into one or two casual get-togethers. But whoever you are, there's a Schedule. Thus, as the evening wears on, you're increasingly thinking, "Okay, this is Date X, which means that, sooner or later, we should be doing Physical Activity Y." And this assumption prompts a whole flurry of mental activity ("what if he does...", "what if she doesn't...", "should I...", "should I not..."), culminating in the big question (which is a question usually only for the woman): "Do I want to?"

Here's where the major league games begin. If you're the guy (who plays quarterback), the challenge is how and when to make the appropriate move. If you're the girl (who plays receiver), things are trickier. For in this climate of expectations, whatever you do is likely to be read — or misread — as a red or a green light. For example, a young woman who preferred a slower Schedule than many of her peers told me, "When I started dating, I would just be my normal, super-warm self — and suddenly I'd notice a glint in the guy's eye. So I realized I had to curb my natural friendliness if I didn't want it to be 'misinterpreted.' But how do I do that without making him think I'm not interested?" When touch is part of the picture, everything "means" something physical — and that may prevent you from being yourself for fear of what it may "mean."

Furthermore, even saying outright, "I really like you, but I don't want to...," is generally interpreted as part of the game (as, indeed, it often is). A guy may assume, "Okay — she's playing 'try and change my mind.' " A girl may assume, "Okay — he's playing 'let's see if I can lower her defenses.' " In other words, up-front statements are rarely taken seriously. As a friend once told me, "The nicest thing a guy ever said to me on a date was, 'I want you know, I don't have any expectations about where this will lead — I just enjoy being with you.' But even then, I didn't believe him."

The bottom line is, the only way to avoid game-playing is to avoid physicality. Only then can you accomplish the most important step in forming a relationship and, at the same time, enjoy one of life's greatest pleasures: really getting to know someone.

Agreeing not to touch does even more to bring about a genuine relationship. In particular, it helps you identify the object of all your warm feelings. Of course, you assume it's the other person. But once you start touching, it's often yourself.

A rabbi I know puts it this way: "I want to tell you something," he'll say to a group of students. "I love chicken. My wife makes the greatest chicken. I don't know what she does to it, but it comes out really tasty, and I love it. But does that mean I love *the* chicken? Of course not. If I did, I wouldn't want to eat it! I'd want to put a sweater on it, make sure it's not cold in the winter, take good care of it. So when I say, 'I love chicken,' what am I really saying? I'm saying that I love the way *I feel* when I eat chicken. In other words, 'I love chicken' means I love *myself*."

Then he'll turn to a girl in the class. "Now, let me ask you something," he'll say with a smile.

"When a guy says 'I love you' — which kind of love does he mean?"

Touch feels good — even better than eating chicken. When touch enters a relationship before a deeper bond has developed, the wonderful sensation you experience may seem like love for the other person when in fact it is nothing more than loving how wonderful you feel being with him or her — or, put more bluntly, self-love.

Ultimately, refraining from touching leads to a much deeper connection than is otherwise likely. I could say more about this, but instead I'll let Andy do the talking.

I met Andy, a young man in his middle twenties, on a Discovery seminar. I appreciated his presence in my class — he asked several good questions and seemed to be taking in everything quite intently. Afterwards we spoke briefly, and he impressed me as being exceptionally intelligent and sensitive. I later heard that he was staying on to do more learning, and my husband, who had also met him, was betting that he was on his way to becoming religious.

One afternoon not long after our first meeting, Andy showed up at my door.

"I feel like I owe you this visit," he said, looking pretty serious, "because something amazing has happened to me during the past two weeks, and it's got to do with what you were saying in your class."

"This sounds intriguing," I said with a grin. "Let's hear about it."

"First of all," Andy said, "in case I didn't tell you before, everything you said about dating made a lot of sense. Of course, I wasn't exactly ready to put it all into practice — especially the part about no physical contact — but I have to admit I heard the logic in it."

He took a deep breath.

"Anyway, a couple of weeks ago, I happened to meet this girl named Deborah. She had become religious back in the States last year and came here to learn more. She seemed very bright and friendly, and so, being curious about all of this, I asked her how and why she had gotten into Judaism. We started talking. I was very impressed with her. We ended up talking for two hours. It was great. We really connected.

"Now, I want to tell you something. I wasn't even interested in this girl at first. To be honest, her looks didn't do much for me. And I couldn't even tell what she looked like under that potato-sack dress she was wearing."

I stifled a laugh. I could guess what style Andy was referring to, popular among moms-to-be.

"But I really liked her as a person. And because she was religious, there was no physical contact at all. It was weird for me not to be able to touch her even casually — not even a pat on the back — but I respected where she was coming from. We spoke more the next day for about six hours. About all kinds of stuff. And also the next day. And the day after that.

"Two weeks have gone by now, and we've spent I don't know how many hours together. On Shabbat, we stayed up till five o'clock in the morning just talking and being with each other, and even then neither of us wanted to stop. And all this time, I swear I haven't so much as touched her hand.

"You know," he continued with just the faintest tinge of embarrassment, "I'm not bragging or anything, but I'm pretty much a 'ladies' man.' I've always gone out with a lot of really attractive women, basically whomever I wanted. You should've seen my last girlfriend. She was a knockout. And I guess I don't have to tell you that my relationships weren't exactly 'hands off.' I suppose most of them also weren't so deep.

"But now, for the first time, the exact opposite has happened. Like I said, in the beginning I didn't even find this girl especially attractive. It was her mind and personality I was taken with. But now I'm crazy about her looks, too. Here, let me show you a picture I took of her. I carry it with me all the time. Isn't she cute?"

Andy withdrew a photograph from his shirt pocket, gazed at it with feeling, and handed it to me. It featured a smiling girl, average in appearance. I also couldn't tell what she looked like under her "potato-sack" dress.

"She's cute," I agreed.

He beamed, glancing at the picture again before returning it to his pocket.

"But that's not the main thing," Andy continued, pausing as if he himself needed a moment to digest the realization he was about to share. "What's really incredible is that I have never respected a woman so much in my life. And I've never felt so much for anyone in such a short time. I can honestly say I love her. I know," he hastened to add, not wanting to lose credibility, "it must be nothing compared to the love you feel after being married for a few years. But still," he said emphatically, leaning forward, "there's no question in my mind that this is not infatuation. It's the real thing. When — I mean if — I become religious, I want to marry this girl. And I still don't know what she looks like under that baggy dress. And I don't even care."

Wow, I thought. Another Marlboro Man bites the dust. My girlfriends and I have always agreed that one of the most convincing proofs of Torah is its ability to turn guys into menschen.

"I just wanted to tell you all this," Andy concluded, "because I am blown away. You guys have something really powerful going here. What do you call it — *shomer negiah*? Well, I'll tell you, this stuff is the strongest love potion around."

As he headed down the stairs, he turned to me. "You know what?" he said. "You should bottle this stuff and sell it. I'm not kidding."

CHAPTER FOUR

Going for the Best

I remember an interesting conversation I had with someone many years ago. It was during my first trip back to the U.S. after having quite unpredictably become religious in Israel. Among the old friends and acquaintances I called was 24-year-old Rick, whom I had met the previous year. Rick, to put it mildly, did not have a highly spiritual lifestyle or very deep relationships with women. Yet for everything I found distasteful about him (and everything he thought was weird about me, like my pursuit of a meaningful life), we had always connected intellectually and often got into intense discussions.

On this occasion, the main topic was physical relationships. Rick simply could not understand how I could possibly be willing, at some future date, to marry someone I had never touched. It was absurd. It was insane. Either I'd been brainwashed, or I was off my rocker.

"Rick," I interrupted, "let me ask you something. Have you ever had a purely friendly relationship with a woman that only much later turned romantic?"

He thought for a moment. "Yeah," he said. "Once."

"Well," I continued, "the first time it got physical, didn't it feel different from being with other women? Didn't it mean a lot more?"

There was a pause on the other end of the line.

"Yeah," he conceded slowly. "It did."

"Well," I said, "I'll be doing the same thing. But because I'll be taking it even further, I'm going to get even more out of it."

More silence. I felt I had touched something (figuratively speaking).

"Okay, I get it," he said.

Another pause.

Then he volunteered, "You know, when I meet a woman I really like — I mean, when there's really something there — I almost don't want the relationship to get physical too soon. I feel like that would ruin it."

Not only do we in the religious Jewish world not want to "ruin" a relationship, we want to get the most out of it. We want to get the most out of all of life. The majority of people would probably agree with Judaism that "most" has to do with quality, not quantity; with depth, not breadth. In other words, people really want not the most out of life but the *best*. They would pass up numerous average enjoyments in favor of a few really deep ones. Nowhere is this truer than in relationships. At bottom, most sensitive individuals want one lifelong partner with whom they can feel the intense pleasure of uniqueness and singularity that is called — specialness.

Judaism wants relationships to be special. True specialness results when two people experience something together that neither has experienced before. Of course, specialness begins with emotion. The more exclusive your feelings toward each other, the more unique your union. And since your physical relationship draws so much of its strength from those feelings, the more singular and intense they are, the more powerful such intimacy — starting with touch — will be. But it can go farther, into a realm that Rick will unfortunately never experience. For if physical closeness itself is something you have known only with each other, nothing is more special.

I remember something a close friend of mine once told me. Rachel had had a typical secular social life before encountering Judaism in her early twenties. Some time after becoming religious, she found the man she wanted to marry. Throughout their engagement, she and her husband-to-be had strictly adhered to Halachah (Jewish law), and the first time they'd touched was after the *chupah* (wedding ceremony) in the *yichud* room (the private room to which bride and groom retreat immediately after the ceremony). When I was still single, I was very curious about all this (especially the part in the *yichud* room). I asked Rachel what it had been like to finally touch the man with whom she would be spending the rest of her life — and, if she didn't mind my asking (I mean, of course it was none of my business, but still...), what did they do in there anyway??

Rachel grinned at the question and blushed a little but was happy to respond (as I'd figured she would be).

"Well," she said, obviously savoring the memory, "I can't speak for other people. I imagine they probably can't wait to hug and kiss each other. But for us, the feeling was so intense that neither of us felt the need to do that — at least not right away. For a long time, we just held hands and stood there gazing at each other."

I looked at her incredulously. You wait however many months to finally touch the person you're marrying, and then, when that moment comes, you stand there holding hands?! But once my initial shock subsided, I understood — that simple touch was so incredible because it was the first time both Rachel and her husband had ever felt so much for anyone. And suddenly, I knew how much they each must have wished, thinking back on that day (and that night): "If only *everything* were the first time...."

We all want specialness. Yet even something earthshakingly wonderful in your first romantic relationship will feel more commonplace a few people down the line. With each involvement, your sensitivity is dulled. As a result, that ultimate relationship will be less special. So why do most people enter into physical relationships they know may not last, chipping away at the potential for later experiencing that highest "high" of all?

The answers are many. First, judging by my experience in *kiruv*, I would say that many people probably reach their deathbeds without ever pondering what the best in life is, never mind how to get it. Second, even a thinking person most likely won't consider an option that seems completely foreign, no matter how much sense it may make. (Would *Cosmopolitan* ever suggest not getting heavily physical with a guy until you're married to him??) Third, even if he or she would contemplate such an option, society doesn't make it easy to swim upstream. There's almost uncombatable pressure to be "normal," whatever the current definition happens to be. (In the secular world, it can be unbearably embarrassing to reach a prescribed age without having certain experiences under your belt. As a result, many people have their first — and not especially moving — sexual encounter not because "it was the right person" but because, as someone once told me with a shrug, "it was time.") Finally, and most obviously, not everyone self-confident enough to be different can resist immediate gratification, even when it's minuscule compared to the pleasure he or she is sacrificing in the long run.

"Winning" in life, therefore, requires a clear understanding of your goal, a strategy for achieving it, the courage of your convictions, and self-discipline. Armed with these strengths, in addition to a single-minded desire for the best in life, you wouldn't compromise. You wouldn't just say, "What the heck? So I'll fool around now and sacrifice some uniqueness later with the person I'll be spending the rest of my life with. Whatever specialness is left is good enough for me."

Judaism is not alone in advocating the pursuit of life's deepest pleasures. What makes Judaism unique is that it doesn't just pay lip service to this ideal ("Well, yeah, I guess I do want things to be special, but..."). It insists that you accept nothing less. In asking you to refrain from physical involvement now for the sake of that ultimate relationship, Judaism is directing you towards the best life has to offer.

CHAPTER FIVE

Injuries, Scars, and the Self-Fulfilling Prophecy

Human beings are exceedingly vulnerable. One fall on your face and you may need stitches. One wrong turn on your skis and you may find yourself with a broken leg. Thankfully, your body works naturally to heal itself, but even with proper medical attention you may end up scarred or disabled.

The same is true of your emotions. A childhood trauma may reverberate throughout your adult life, and even recent hurts may take years to fade. As fragile as you are physically, you are often even more so emotionally.

Once, as I introduced myself and my topic to a Discovery group, I noticed a deadly serious look on the face of one woman in the room. I began as I always do, saying that the religious approach to dating is designed in part to discourage emotional investment in doomed relationships. The woman sat back in her chair, arms folded, wearing a tight, pained expression. I gave an example of such a dead-end relationship, in which only one partner sought a long-term commitment. Her face darkened and she nodded almost imperceptibly. "Hmm," I thought. "Seems like this must have happened to her." I gave a second example, that of a relationship that eventually and painfully terminated because the partners' life goals did not coincide. She looked more miserable still, sighed heavily and nodded again, this time quite visibly. "Oy," I wondered, "this, too?" I felt hesitant about continuing, but I didn't have much choice. So I took a deep breath and gave my final example: an unhealthy relationship. I wasn't prepared for what happened next: her eyes filled with tears, she got up, and walked out.

This woman was in considerable pain. Had her suffering been physical, she probably would have been hospitalized. Then again, had she anticipated such great physical distress, she would have been much more cautious to begin with.

Most people are quite wary of physical risks. They will not, for example, jump off a diving board without knowing if there is water in the pool below. Feelings, on the other hand, are intangible. Emotional dangers are therefore far more difficult to identify and take seriously.

The sad truth is that because of the subtlety of emotional damage, countless people throw caution to the winds, dive into empty pools, and then walk around with the equivalent of open wounds and fractured limbs. Most of these victims don't even realize the extent of their injuries. Yet one's heart suffers as surely as one's body. And although time may heal all wounds, the scars remain.

If an angel were to visit you in the womb and offer you anything you desired, one of the most priceless blessings you could request would be a positive outlook on life. Some people are born with it, good parenting can go a long way toward implanting it, and you may even be able to learn it. But much depends on your experiences.

Since relationships are so central to our lives, they largely determine our outlook. When you succeed in a relationship, you feel good about life. But every time you get clobbered emotionally, hopelessness sets in, leading you to conclude that such optimism is only for the foolish or the blind.

I once had a brief encounter with a very unhappy 18-year-old girl. Dawn had been heavily involved with a number of guys who, one after the other, had come and gone in her life. When I met her, she had just followed her latest boyfriend to Israel. Shortly after she'd arrived, he'd broken up with her. She was in despair. It pained me to hear her speak.

"I've had it with relationships!" she said tearfully, her shockingly deep bitterness cutting into me like a knife. "I never want to have anything to do with men again as long as I live."

I'm sure other teenage girls have mouthed similar sentiments following a breakup. But I had never seen such utter disillusionment in a person her age. I felt as if I were listening to a jaded older woman who'd divorced a succession of abusive and unfaithful men. Yet Dawn had barely reached adulthood. Had she grown up in a different environment, she might have retained a positive and trusting perspective on life and relationships. I knew I was witnessing a tragedy that needn't have happened.

If we want not only healthy limbs and organs but healthy psyches, we have to treat our souls as carefully as our bodies. We have to be just as wary of emotional cliffs as physical ones, and we have to understand how easily we can step over the edge.

Few areas of life involve more emotional intensity, and therefore greater risk, than male-female relationships. When you become involved with someone, you let down the self-protective barrier you erect in your dealings with others. You put your emotions on the line. You allow yourself to be vulnerable. Even with touch out of the picture, you've got a lot to lose. But add the powerful bond created by physical closeness, and immeasurably more is at stake.

Each time a relationship breaks up, you pay a price. You grow less confident in your ability to distinguish reality from fantasy. You lose faith in the permanence of relationships and the goodness of others, particularly the opposite sex. And in the end, you forfeit the optimism essential to happiness.

This defeat is sad enough. But here a vicious circle can be set in motion. The next time you meet someone, you are already on your guard. You no longer trust enough to become close. The other person, in turn, may sense your closedness and back out of the relationship, dealing your trust yet another blow. You then retreat deeper into your protective shell, further dimming the prospect of future success. Disillusionment thus gives rise to fatalism, which becomes a self-fulfilling prophecy.

One of the most effective strategies for not getting hurt is not bonding with another person until it is safe to do so. Reserving physical closeness for the security of a permanent relationship helps safeguard your happiness — and your future.

CHAPTER SIX

We Women Are from Venus — and Remind Me Where Men Are from Again...?

WARNING: I realize that gender differences are a hot topic. If you bristle when people generalize about men and women, this chapter is guaranteed to push your button. Read it anyway.

I was once walking through the Old City when a young man stopped me for directions. Suddenly his eyes narrowed, and he asked me suspiciously, "Hey, wait a minute — aren't you Gila Manolson, who wrote *The Magic Touch*?"

Apparently he had heard me speak somewhere. "Yup, that's me," I replied with a cheerful smile.

He didn't look cheerful at all. "You should know," he informed me, "that there's a 'contract' out on you for writing that book!"

Gee, I thought. Lots of girls told me they liked it....

With that introduction, I'd like to interject a brief word about differences between the sexes. As warned, I'll be making generalizations (many guys actually did like my book), but I believe they're valid — and while you've probably heard them before, they're worth remembering. Finally, while this chapter focuses on women, any man who cares about others should find it just as relevant.

Meanwhile, for those who may not grasp why I rank high on many guys' Most Wanted List, the following story should make it clear.

I was giving my dating class to about sixty 18-year-old men from modern-Orthodox homes. Until then I had lectured only in all-female or coed settings. As usual, I wanted to start by contrasting secular dating with its Jewish, marriage-oriented counterpart.

"Why do secular teenagers date?" I asked.

Some guilty looks were exchanged.

"Okay," I said. "Let me change the question. I assume that, although no one here is thinking about marriage yet, most of you are dating. So tell me — why do you date?"

Absolute silence. I noticed, however, that the guilty looks had become secretive grins.

Hmm, I thought. I wouldn't have expected this group to be shy. "Come on," I prodded them. "Why do you date?"

The same conspiratorial silence. More secretive grins.

What's with these guys? I wondered. Whenever I asked this question of women, they had no difficulty answering:

"It's fun."

"Curiosity."

"Everyone's doing it."

"Because you're attracted."

"So you won't be lonely."

"To have someone to feel close to."

This was my first all-male audience and the first time I had gotten this mysterious reaction. Suddenly I realized what was going on and what my listeners needed to hear.

"Okay, guys," I said. "Let's get real. Nothing you say is going to shock me. So just tell me the truth: Why do you date?"

One brave soul raised his hand and said, with a big grin, "To score!" A wave of relieved laughter spread through the room, expressing the consensus.

That's an answer no woman has ever given me. A woman may say, "Hormones." But "to score" reflects a particularly male attitude towards dating. As a 30-something woman reasonably attuned to reality, I knew how males think. Yet it had taken a long, mystifying silence on the part of these sixty young men before I recalled it. Had no one been honest, I probably would have just assumed they were a quiet group, and continued obliviously along.

Which just goes to show you: We women never learn. Somewhere in our brains, we've stored the information that men aren't like us, but we often fail to access it. Maybe it's an intellectual block: We can't comprehend how another human being could possibly operate on such a dissimilar plane. Maybe it's an emotional block: We so want to believe that men relate to us exactly as we relate to them — or at least that "this one's different." Either way, we suffer from recurrent amnesia.

The fact is, in relationships, males are wired to be focused more on the physical. And females are wired to forget this.

Furthermore, "scoring" usually means something beyond whatever a girl has in mind. The well-known rabbi Dovid Orlofsky puts it this way:

"No guy," he'll tell a group of skeptical young women, "has ever walked down the street holding a girl's hand, thinking, 'Ahh. Completion. I feel so satisfied and content just holding her hand!' And no guy has ever seen a beautiful woman walk by and said to himself, 'Wow. I'd sure like to hold her hand!' Get this through your heads!!" (The old Beatles' song "I Wanna Hold Your Hand" was such a hit precisely because women fell for it.)

Needless to say, this is nothing new. Fifteen hundred years ago, the Talmud (*Ketubot* 64b), in its typically straightforward style, described the difference between male and female sexuality in the following statement: "Go out and learn from the prostitutes' marketplace. Who's hiring whom?" In other words, men have historically paid for an experience that, for most women, wouldn't be worth it.

But there's more. The Talmud then sums it up: "His drive comes from the outside, hers from the inside."

Both men and women have hormones. But the average woman can't relate to a man totally externally. To become physically involved, she has to feel something more. He doesn't.

A teacher I know once made this point in the following way:

"Ladies," she addressed the female half of the

class, "imagine this: You're in a restaurant when an absolutely gorgeous guy comes in and sits down at the table next to you. He opens his mouth — and you hear him say something really stupid. A minute later he opens his mouth again — and again he says something really stupid. Suddenly, his attractiveness has plummeted, and any relationship you may have fantasized about having with him has gone up in smoke. Am I right?"

Vigorous nods.

"Now, guys," she continued, "you're in a restaurant when an incredibly beautiful woman comes in and sits down at the table next to you. She opens her mouth — and says something really stupid. She opens her mouth again — and again she says something really stupid. And a third time. And a fourth, and a fifth. You may not want to marry her — but I bet she's still looking just as good."

Guilty grins.

If every guy with little to offer besides his looks would obligingly say something stupid right away, as in the above example, women would be a lot better off. Unfortunately, this doesn't always happen. And here we arrive at the key point: In addition to forgetting how men work, women are blessed with fertile and eager imaginations. Consequently, as long as an attractive guy isn't saying stupid things, a woman will invest him with all sorts of imaginary virtues so she can feel better about where her hormones are taking her. (And once she's gotten there, any stupid remarks he makes will probably sound cute.)

The upshot is that women are more prone to this type of self-delusion than men, and inevitably suffer the consequences. If you're a woman, you will be more likely to want to see something, believe you see it, and, based on this illusion, devote yourself physically and emotionally to someone about as appropriate for you as King Kong. And in the end, when it doesn't work out, and he says, "Thanks, it's been fun, and I hope you didn't take things too seriously," you're the one who gets hurt.

I know you guys don't have it easy, either. Just as a woman's need for connection puts her at a disadvantage emotionally, a man's testosterone levels put him at a disadvantage biologically. To put it bluntly, you probably want something from women more than they want to give it. As a result, you may often feel compelled to figure out what the heck women want and then adapt to their wishes (at least on the outside) in an attempt to secure a relationship. I've never been a guy, so I can't speak from experience, but it must be pretty frustrating.

No less real, however, is the damage you sustain when you encourage a woman's emotional involvement in a less than serious relationship. Though you may not be intentionally "leading her on" or "using her," that is what's happening. The cost to you is diminished sensitivity to other people's feelings and realities — a trait likely to manifest itself in other areas of life and keep you from becoming as caring a person as you could be.

So I want to conclude with a plea to both sexes: Be careful. Women, realize that you're more vulnerable than you think. And men, realize that women suffer tremendously by being unable to sideline their emotions. The safest route is to keep a relationship non-physical. Without physicality, a woman will have less reason to delude herself, and a man will have less reason to let her. Being *shomer negiah* protects a woman's heart — and a man's sensitivity.

CHAPTER SEVEN

In Defense of Not Knowing What You're Missing (or "Ignorance Is Bliss")

I f you've read this far, you may agree with some or even all of what I've said. Still, you might feel that, in holding off until marriage, you're losing out on something significant — that passing up physical relationships now means "giving up" something real.

Once, when I was addressing a group of young women from observant homes on the value of being *shomer negiah*, one girl who had been staring at me stonily for some time suddenly interrupted.

"Easy for you to say," she retorted. "People who weren't brought up religious have had their fun. We haven't!"

"Right!" a second girl chimed in, and before I knew it, there was a whole chorus of women complaining in unison.

The spokesperson of the group summed it up.

"You don't understand," she said. "We don't even know what we're missing!"

They all waited to hear what I had to say to that.

"That's exactly my point," I responded. "In the long run, you're not missing anything. Not only that, but you're going to come out ahead."

Uncomprehending silence. How could this be??

People are often led into less-than-ultimate relationships by an unconscious worship of Experience. In a relatively wholesome society, this attitude may mean seeing physical involvement before marriage as essential to personal growth and development. In the world at large, many take the Experience Principle to the extreme, assuming that the more they sample anything and everything life has to offer, the broader, worldlier, and more enriched they become. Inexperience is equated with losing out. The fact is, there's a lot more to be said for remaining innocent.

I know innocence hasn't been touted as a virtue for some time now. Particularly for secular teenagers, popularity and innocence don't generally go hand in hand. I remember back in tenth grade, a "test" was circulated in which you scored points for your lack of innocence in sexual activity, drug use, and so on, starting one step up from infant-like inexperience and progressing to the dizzying heights of really mature, glamorously self-destructive behavior. The scoring went something like: 0-5 = "pure as the driven snow" — an insufferable embarrassment; 6-10 = "still a babe in arms"; 11-20 = "losing your naiveté"; 21-30 =

"on your way to getting messed up"; 31-50 = "messed up"; and over 50 = the coveted "really messed up." Some people scored so low that they secretly added on ten to twenty points so they could report a respectable total. Meanwhile, those who could get away with it were nonchalantly awarding themselves "75s," and still others were boasting scores that I doubt even the entire Rolling Stones could match.

Admittedly, the intensity of such juvenile claims to "sophistication" fades after adolescence. And today, with the appearance of such cheerful phenomena as the AIDS epidemic and widespread substance addiction, some trends have even begun to reverse themselves to the point where conservatism is socially acceptable (as long as you're still "cool"). But while certain vices are no longer glorified, the mystique of worldliness lingers. Experience is still the name of the game.

Obviously, to live is to experience. Yet Judaism urges that experimentation not take place indiscriminately and for its own sake. Experiencing should be a highly selective means to a lofty end: becoming a better, more spiritually sensitive, and ultimately happier person.

I assume that, unlike some secular teenagers, most individuals raised in even mildly wholesome homes are not aspiring to a life of sex, drugs, and rock 'n' roll. Yet whatever attraction you may feel to something "out there," even something as seemingly innocent as a nice little physical relationship, could very well be a tamer manifestation of that same desire to not "miss out." The temptation to "broaden" oneself through some apparently harmless experience is particularly alluring, and many have fallen for it. Do yourself a big favor. Don't get sucked in.

If you still have doubts, ask a few sensitive and sincere *ba'alei teshuvah* (people who returned to Judaism as adults) whether, if given the chance to live their lives over, they would change anything. I've watched a lot of people grow in Torah, from their first steps till they've "settled in," and I've seen the same evolution of thought among them all, culminating in an almost universal conclusion.

When people are very new to Judaism, they'll often say: "I'm glad I've come to Torah at this time in my life and not earlier. I wouldn't want to have missed many of the things I've done up till now. I wouldn't trade those great experiences for anything."

Later, their perspective on the past changes somewhat. They'll say, "I wish I hadn't done everything I did before becoming religious. I mean, I did gain from some of my experiences, and I know I have an understanding and appreciation of Judaism that I wouldn't have otherwise. But it sure would have been nicer if I could have learned what I did straight from Torah and skipped all that stuff."

Later still, particularly after they're married, the refrain will have evolved into something like: "Ugh, when I think of some of the things I did before getting into Judaism! I know God must have had His reasons for making me go that route. But I would give anything to have been brought up religious. Thank God, my kids won't have to go through what I did." (Too bad only hindsight is 20/20.)

Nowhere is this rejection of the Experience Principle stronger than in relationships. Why? First and foremost, there's the big, big issue of forfeited sensitivity and singularity, as we've discussed. Each previous involvement lingering in one's memory dilutes the specialness with one's husband or wife that we all so intensely desire.

I once spoke with someone who felt this loss more acutely than anyone I'd ever met. After my class on dating, a young woman asked if she could speak to me privately.

"I consider myself a good, religious girl," she began, "and I've always been *shomer negiah*. This year I started dating. A few weeks ago I began going out with a boy who's very nice, but not quite as religious as I am. We really like each other, and we've been getting closer. Recently, he started saying that it's getting so hard for him to be *shomer negiah* with me. He said he knows I am and respects me for it, but he still really wants to kiss me."

Here it comes, I said to myself. True Confessions.

"Well," she continued, a blush of shame rising to her cheeks, "last week, one evening, we were out walking in a park...and there weren't really any people around...and it felt very romantic...and all of a sudden — he kissed me. And I let him." She looked down in embarrassment.

Judging by her tone of voice, the experience hadn't been unpleasant. Good, I thought. She's normal.

There was a long pause. When she raised her head again, her face wore a pathetic expression.

"And now..." she said sadly, "now...I feel like — used merchandise!"

As her words registered, I had two reactions. "Honey," my pre-religious inner voice replied incredulously, "you feel like 'used merchandise' — and all you did is kiss someone?? You must be part of some nearly extinct species!" At the same time, my present religious personality thought sadly, "Poor girl. She's right." And my heart went out to her.

This young woman's words were very precious to me. In a world where everything means so little, she knew she had lost something, because her husband would no longer be the first man she'd kiss. Some people may think this is sweet. Others may think it's ludicrous. I think it's enviable. Because if she's so sensitive to what she's lost, then once she's married, she's going to be just as sensitive to everything she has. And that's something that "experience" can't hold a candle to.

Another source of disenchantment with the Experience Principle is the unpleasant tendency toward comparisons. As important as objectivity is when you're dating, subjectivity is what it's all about once you're married. Ideally, you'll want to feel that no one can possibly measure up to your unbelievably wonderful husband or wife. Yet each premarital relationship opens the door wider to innumerable comparisons between your spouse and some past boyfriend or girlfriend. And, needless to say (since your husband or wife will probably not compare favorably in every respect, no matter how fabulous he or she is), such evaluations don't do either one of you — or your relationship — any good.

A woman named Chana, who used to teach in Discovery, once shared with me a remark made by someone in her class. Chana had just pointed out that the absence of past partners with whom to compare your spouse strengthens your marriage, while memories can only make for problems. Immediately a man (whose wife I assume was not present) volunteered (and publicly, no less) the following delightful comment:

"I know what you mean. I've been married for two years, and I really love my wife, but — especially in our most intimate moments — I can't help thinking about my previous girlfriend."

When Chana told me that, I cringed. If I were that man's wife and overheard what he said, I'd be devastated. And every time I quote him in my classes, the looks I get from my students indicate that I am not alone. The nearly unanimous reaction is: UGH. (The people who don't respond with "ugh" are usually looking distinctly uncomfortable, apparently having thought something along the same lines as this man.)

Unfortunately, people don't realize the lifelong impact of their experience. An 18-year-old yeshivah (religious school) student once demonstrated this shortsightedness:

"I have a two-stage approach to dating," he explained. "Stage One is, I'm 18 and not thinking about getting married, so I'm going to have fun — if you know what I mean. Stage Two will be when I'm, say, 22 or 23 and ready for marriage. Then I'll play by the rules. I'll find a good girl, be *shomer negiah,* and reap all the benefits you talk about. In other words," he concluded triumphantly, "I'm going to 'have my cake and eat it, too'!"

When I presented this philosophy to a class of young women, they were incensed. "What kind of garbage is that?" they demanded. "He gets some pure girl, and she gets some guy who's fooled around with all those other women?? That's not fair!!"

Before they could go out and burn this guy in effigy, I told them how I had responded. For his outlook wasn't just "unfair." This young man was totally unaware of the utter fallacy in his "best of both worlds" logic.

"Forgive me for bursting your bubble," I had told him, "but you don't realize something. When you get to Stage Two, you'll no longer be the person you would have been without Stage One. You're going to enter marriage with a storehouse of memories of past girlfriends and a grossly eroded sensitivity. Now that you've 'had your cake,' it won't be there to 'eat' anymore. There's no going back. You've blown it. Get it?"

In short, his approach may have cheated the woman he would someday marry, but it was just as unfair — if not more so — to himself.

The truth is, once they find their soulmate, most people don't exactly relish their memories of past involvements. Nonetheless, such recollections stick with you, surfacing when you least want them to. Someone I know likened them to flies persistently buzzing around your head. Others would surely add that if a previous relationship was relatively casual, or not very good, the thought of having been physically involved with that person can be positively embarrassing. Probably most committed *ba'alei teshuvah*, once happily married, would be grateful if their past relationships, good and bad alike, could be erased with a wave of their hand. One woman even told me, quite seriously, that if some brain surgeon could remove all her memories of anyone but her husband, she'd go for it.

The mistake in thinking you're "missing out" should be clear. You're not missing out by not doing something now if later you'll be relieved you didn't do it. When you're happily settled down with your partner for life, you won't regret all those experiences you've "missed." You'll know, with a certainty you've never had, that the only thing you've missed is what lies ahead.

CHAPTER EIGHT

"But..."

Many people, upon hearing the arguments for holding off on all physical closeness with the opposite sex until marriage, experience a powerful conflict between their intellect and their emotions. Most mature and thinking individuals admit that the idea makes a lot of sense. However, the thought of actually doing such a thing leaves them in a state akin to terror. For some, the prospect conjures up such soothing images as that of jumping off a cliff and into a pool of icy water. For others, even casually entertaining the notion may produce a full-fledged anxiety attack. (Reported symptoms include shortness of breath, a tight feeling in the chest, and temporary paralysis.)

But joking aside: While nearly all resistance to the Jewish approach to relationships stems not from intellectual objections but from "fear of the foreign," secular people in particular generally raise a few valid issues, which deserve to be addressed. The following are the questions most commonly asked.

A Compatibility Gamble?

Q. How do you know the two of you will be physically compatible if you haven't tried things out first?

In phrasing this question, I've deliberately avoided specifying a level of physical intimacy. That's because you can define "things" however you like, based upon your own lifestyle, and both question and answer will still be the same. Way back when young men and women were accustomed to marrying while still fairly innocent, people probably wondered, "How could you marry someone you haven't kissed?" In the '50s, when the intimacy permitted for a college-age "good girl" was "everything but" (with a serious boyfriend), the question undoubtedly was "How could you marry someone you haven't fooled around with?" Today, of course, the norm is to do everything with anybody, not to mention anyone you're actually considering marrying. Accordingly, the question now incredulously asked by many is, "How could you possibly marry someone you haven't had a total physical relationship with??"

What I'm trying to point out, just as a prefatory observation, is that there's nothing objective about the "need" to experience whatever it is with one's future spouse. It is simply a matter of mores. Back in the '50s, the average unmarried girl felt no great anxiety about being good, and the average guy wasn't uptight about marrying her. Even without intimate knowledge of each other, men and women evidently felt secure in their choice of marriage partners. And people were probably no less secure when they abided by a societal norm of even less premarital experience, or none at all. So why must so many people today "try things out," be it anything from just kissing to much more, before committing themselves?

"Ah," the skeptic may interrupt, "but did those old-time innocents have decent physical relationships once they were married? Given the stigma of divorce back then, probably a lot of frustrated people simply resigned themselves to being stuck for life with someone who, they found out too late, had all the sensual sophistication of a buffalo."

In other words, past generations, poor things, weren't given the socially sanctioned opportunity to collect essential data about a potential spouse and undoubtedly suffered the consequences. We, living in these fortunate and enlightened times, have access to such information, so why not get it and profit?

Yet the popular need to "try things out" derives from much more than unwillingness to forfeit this golden opportunity. The fact is, nearly all of us are victims, to one degree or another, of modern society's unnatural, unhealthy attitude towards sexuality.

To a secular person this last statement will sound oddly reversed. "Wait a minute," he or she will object. "We're the ones with the healthy view of sexuality. We feel free to express ourselves with anyone we want. It's religious people who make it into something unnatural with all your dos and don'ts. How can you say we're off?"

I can say it because it seems pretty clear that the current secular approach to sexuality reflects a grave misunderstanding of human nature. As a result, it is failing dismally in producing large numbers of deeply happy and fulfilled human beings.

Modern society's fatal error lies in relating to the body independently of the spirit that animates it. This unfortunate phenomenon is particularly observable in the field of medicine, where doctors often treat the body with little or no regard for the soul, not realizing how much one's mental and spiritual state affects physical health.

Judaism views people in their wholeness. Body and soul are meant to work together as one, with the soul defining one's identity and the body reflecting it. Only then can we be ourselves.

With this holistic perspective, we can draw a basic conclusion about sexuality: Physical intimacy devoid of emotional intimacy is not a true expression of self. Yet many naively assume that we *can* divorce body from soul. We're supposedly able to shove our cumbersome emotions (e.g., "I don't really feel so much for him/her") into the closet and sail onto the streets as liberated bodies, without feeling we've left our real selves at home. In many circles, this body-soul division has become so accepted that one can ask equally casually, "How good a tennis player are you?" and "How good a kisser are you?", without sensing the essential incongruity of the two questions. This is because sexuality altogether has come to be viewed as something purely physical, unrelated to the spirit — an activity that, like sports, can be coldly rated in terms of performance.

We can now understand why people are so afraid to make a lifelong commitment to someone whose ability to "perform" looms as a big question mark. After all, would you commit to a lifelong game of doubles tennis with a partner whom you'd never seen hold a racket?

The crucial mistake, of course, lies in this extremely unrealistic (not to mention crass) comparison. The physical side of a relationship, whatever form it takes, is neither a sport nor a performance subject to a point-basis evaluation by some critic observing from the sidelines. It is a primary means of self-expression and cannot be viewed in isolation from the person as a whole.

In short, to those who defend the popular outlook on sexuality, I would reply that turning people into virtual split personalities is neither natural nor healthy.

At this point in a Discovery seminar, what I'm saying is usually ringing true. I then take a tack that lets people answer the original question for themselves.

"What do you think," I ask, "makes for a good physical relationship?"

People immediately volunteer answers:

"Trust."

"Caring."

"Communication."

"Feeling really connected and close."

"Wanting to make the other person happy."

"Most of you seem to feel," I suggest, "that the main ingredient is emotion."

There are nods.

"Anything else?"

Invariably, someone (often the person who asked the question to begin with) adds with a grin, "Technique."

Grins of agreement spread across many other faces as well.

"Okay. Now I'm going to describe two scenarios. Tell me which one you'd rather be stuck in.

"In scenario number one, you decide to marry someone with whom you've been intimately involved throughout your relationship. Physically, you know exactly what you'll be getting and what you have to give. On the other hand, you've sacrificed considerable objectivity about your partner, and various non-physical aspects of your relationship have never developed half as much as they might have.

"Now you're married, and you have the satisfying physical relationship you expected. But you're starting to see certain things about your spouse that you haven't noticed before, or have overlooked. Eventually you realize that deeply ingrained aspects of his or her personality really bother or even upset you, and that he or she lacks qualities that you can't imagine living the rest of your life without. This realization, in turn, begins to diminish your satisfaction with your intimate life, since beneath the physical pleasure, you don't feel as close and connected as you once did. That's scenario number one."

I pause. There is usually silence as the looks on many people's faces tell me that (even without having been married) they know this scenario.

"Here's scenario number two," I continue. "You decide to marry someone with whom you've had no physical contact. Largely because of this approach, you've been able to maintain a great deal of perspective on who he or she is, and the relationship has had a lot of space to develop deeply on the intellectual, emotional, and spiritual levels. On the other hand, you don't know what to expect physically from either your spouse or, if you are inexperienced, yourself.

"Now you're married, and as you had anticipated, your spiritual relationship is great and getting better all the time. But your intimate life is not earning a place in the Fireworks Hall of Fame.

"Now, which situation would you rather be in?"

It doesn't take most people much time to choose. "Technique" (and even more basic things) can be learned; personality can't. You can easily teach someone the rudiments of kissing (as well as learn yourself), much like you can tell a friend where and how hard to scratch your back when it itches. But it's virtually impossible to teach someone how to be the person you need him or her to be in order to feel, on a much deeper level, what you want to feel from that kiss.

I'd say that the emotional connection between you and another person will account for at least ninety percent of the pleasure and satisfaction you'll experience in your physical relationship. This connection is based upon your each being the kind of person the other can love. Being lovable usually means having certain universally lovable traits, such as kindness, willingness to give, sensitivity, etc., plus whatever particulars the other needs to feel that special attraction. You don't have to get physical to determine whether this "ninety percent" exists.

The remaining ten percent could be called the "how-to's." These can easily be picked up after marriage by anyone with a healthy attitude towards sexual expression, a desire to please one's spouse, a minimum of intelligence, and a willingness to learn and communicate.

Prior physical knowledge is basically irrelevant to marital success and may even interfere with it. Personal knowledge is what counts. For true physical intimacy is nothing more — or less — than an embodiment of emotional intimacy. Therefore, if your questions about your future spouse have been answered — and you also know who you are — you can relax, because the vast majority of your questions about your future intimate life have been answered as well.

"No Pain, No Gain?"

Q. Isn't the pain of failed relationships essential to growth? Aren't you recommending sheltering people from the real world?

This question can be asked only if one assumes such a thing as "The Real World," some universal social reality in which, among other things, a certain amount of pain is necessary for optimal personal growth.

In fact, "The Real World" is a subjective concept defined by whatever risks, physical and emotional, a person's lifestyle entails. Just as we tend to define a fanatic as anyone more zealous than we are, and a heretic as anyone less, our idea of "The Real World" revolves around our personal reality. If, for example, you come from an upper-middle-class background, you probably regard life in a place like Harlem as something out of a horror movie, while you see a relatively "old-fashioned" group of people such as the Amish as living in an artificial bubble — your own lifestyle being, of course, the most natural and normal one. However, a Harlem teenager would scorn your existence as no more "real" than that of a baby in a playpen, while the Amish would view your society with the same apprehension with which you view Harlem.

Within fairly large parameters, every culture creates its own social reality based on its own values. A culture that values, for instance, sophistication, learning through trial and error, and experiencing emotional pain as the path to maturity will create one kind of existence for its members. A culture that values innocence, sees no point in learning things the hard way, and takes emotional pain very seriously will create a very different kind of existence. The issue is not what constitutes "The Real World" but what any social group wants to constitute *its* real world. Accordingly, the crucial question is not which humanly created existence is more "real," but which is more conducive to emotional health and happiness.

You should be equally skeptical, therefore, about any pronouncements as to how much and what kinds of pain are necessary in life. This determination is just as subjective. While you undoubtedly perceive the suffering of a Harlem teenager as needless, he or she probably wonders how you'll ever mature in your little cocoon. At the same time, the Amish may well pity you for what your society forces you to go through, while you can't imagine how their "cloistered" lifestyle doesn't stunt their growth.

So we have to ask ourselves: How do we know that the pain accompanying secular life is at all necessary?

Of course, whenever I pose this question of Discovery participants, they jump to defend the system. "I would never be the person I am today if I hadn't gotten hurt in life," the refrain usually goes. "Everything I've gone through, I've gained from."

I'm not arguing with the assertion that one (hopefully) learns and grows through suffering. What I am arguing with is the idea that we should therefore put ourselves in situations likely to result in pain. If I were hit by a train and had to spend the next year in a cast from head to toe, I would gain an unmatched appreciation of the frailty and finiteness of the human body. That doesn't mean I'm going to go out and stand on the tracks waiting for the 6:30 local.

Anything learned through pain comes at a price: inevitable and often permanent damage to one's body or — far worse — one's heart. In most cases, we cannot foresee what this price will be, or if it's worth paying, particularly where our emotions are concerned. Too often, the cost far exceeds the benefit.

For example, I assume that even the most liberal-minded mother wouldn't suggest that her daughter give prostitution a try as a learning experience. Likewise, upon discovering her daughter already gainfully employed in the field, this mother would not simply sigh, "Well, I guess it's all part of growing up." The utter self-degradation of prostitution overrides any "educational" value it may have.

Obviously, not all situations are this clear-cut. But that's where we really have to be careful. We've talked about the emotional toll of broken relationships in terms of desensitization and despair. When we get involved in a relationship that seems harmless but is bound to end, are we wise enough to know we'll emerge the better for it rather than the worse?

To the Jewish mind, which cherishes sensitivity and emotional wholeness, many secular "learning experiences" aren't what they're cracked up to be. They're fun and temporarily gratifying but, in the final analysis, simply not worth it. Jewish law therefore shields its adherents from much of the suffering of the secular world. God will make sure we all get the pain we need to grow — no more and no less, and without our seeking it out.

Judaism's approach to relationships is not overprotective — it's simply more intelligent. Which may explain why people are increasingly making the Jewish world their "real world."

How About Once You're Engaged?

Q. If the idea is to wait until you've found the right person and made a commitment, why not get physical once you're engaged?

If Judaism gave engaged couples the green light for physical closeness, the time between meeting someone and getting engaged would shrink considerably, and an unprecedented number of engagements would be taking place (and broken engagements, and new engagements, and new broken engagements...). Because of their normal and powerful desire for physical closeness with a member of the opposite sex, men and women would fool themselves into thinking they'd found the right person so they could become engaged and start experiencing those pleasurable feelings already. The subconscious is quite capable of such tricks, and this one is child's play.

"Well, then," a Discovery participant will pipe up, "if you're worried about people getting engaged just to have a physical relationship, isn't there a risk they'll get *married* for that reason?"

Despite our propensity for self-deception, my response to this question is no. That's because engagement and marriage are very different. Let me illustrate with a story.

In the mid-'70s, society's fever of self-delusion was still running high (having not yet been cooled by the cynicism of the late '80s). Behind our house lived a woman in her early thirties named Anne who had recently divorced her husband. Lately I had noticed a guy in his early twenties hanging out at her place an awful lot. One day I saw him in Anne's backyard, shooting baskets. I went up to the fence separating our yard from hers and started chatting with him.

"I've seen you around here a lot lately," I began innocently. "Have you just moved into the neighborhood?"

"Yeah," he answered nonchalantly. "I'm living with Anne."

As a rather naive 16-year-old, I was a bit taken aback. But being just as upfront, I asked, "Why don't you guys get married?"

Challenged by my bluntness, he apparently decided to educate me. "We don't need to get married," he countered, somewhat defensively. "Living together is the same thing. We know we love each other, and we're committed to each other. We don't need a piece of paper to prove it."

He dribbled the ball a couple of times and shot another basket. "Besides," he added, "I'm not ready to get married yet."

Only later did I catch the contradiction: Living

together is the same as being married, but he's not ready to get married. That's when I realized someone here is kidding himself.

Just as Anne's boyfriend, deep down, knew full well that there's a big difference between being married and living together, we all know there's a big difference between being married and being engaged. Marriage entails legally and spiritually joining with another, deepening your commitment immeasurably. The thought of jumping into the wrong marriage and then having to terminate it generates considerable fear, both conscious and subconscious. Divorce can inflict untold emotional pain and scar not only one's marital record but one's being. Engagement, on the other hand, is a mere verbal agreement, and breaking it is far less serious. While undoubtedly very upsetting, calling off a wedding is simple, quick, and not the end of the world. Never underestimate the power of the subconscious — it is fully aware of this difference.

If all you had to do was get engaged in order to give your hormones free rein, you'd be far more susceptible to confusing them for "the real thing." And then, assuming you did fall victim to this deception, you'd scarcely be better off than if you were dating secularly. You'd face the same risks — sacrifice of objectivity, loss of opportunity for something deeper to develop, a painful breakup, etc. — with the only difference being that you'd had to call yourself "engaged" (as opposed to merely "seeing someone") for the downward spiral to begin. And if you did make it through engagement to marriage, you'd be just as likely to have married the wrong person based upon an illusion.

At bottom, engagement is not a definitive commitment but merely a " 'commitment' to [later] be committed." Only marriage itself, a true and total commitment permeating all levels of the conscious and subconscious, can provide the optimal framework for experiencing physical closeness with fewer risks and greater joy.

Isn't It Asking Too Much?

Q. Doesn't being shomer negiah *conflict with human nature? And even if not, doesn't our society make it virtually impossible?*

Every human being experiences a lifelong, internal battle between two great drives: the urge for immediate gratification, and the desire for far greater pleasure in the long run. Embarrassing as the admission may be, which side wins — and the depth of happiness we consequently experience — usually boils down to one thing: maturity.

After I'd presented all the practical reasons for being *shomer negiah* to a Discovery class, a 21-year-old guy raised his hand.

"Okay, everything you've said makes sense," he conceded, a challenging grin on his face. "But, I mean, like — hey, come on, isn't it just too hard?"

" 'Just too hard'?" I countered. "What's going to happen when you're in law school and have to choose between partying every night or passing the bar? Are you going to shrug off studying with 'it's just too hard'? Being *shomer negiah* isn't an isolated test. Life is full of instances in which you have to delay gratification — and yes, it's hard. But if you don't learn how to do it, you're going to be a big-time loser."

His smile faded.

"There is, of course," I added, "someone I wouldn't call a loser for wanting something and having to have it now." I turned to the class. "Does anyone know who that is?"

No one had a clue.

I turned back to my questioner, who wore a hopeful expression. Looking at him good and hard, I said, "MY 2-YEAR-OLD!" Whether this guy ever got up the guts to change, I don't know, but he got the message.

No, being *shomer negiah* isn't easy. Many things in life aren't. But if it's worth it, you do it.

This axiom applies no matter when and where you're living. Every era and society poses spiritual challenges. For poor, observant, immigrant Jews in New York around the turn of the last century, the test was keeping Shabbat while still putting food on the table. Every Sunday meant finding new employment after being fired for not showing up on Saturday. If you're not religious, you may not relate. But because some of these people had the inner strength to meet the test, many of their great-great-grandchildren are still Jewish. You may be one of them.

Today, our spiritual challenges are largely moral — and particularly sexual. In the secular world, male-female relationships are going down the tubes, and if we want ours to succeed, we're going to have to conduct our lives differently.

Sadly, many people succumb to helplessness. "It all made so much sense sitting in your class in Jerusalem," a woman wrote me from the States. "But back here, it's another world. I know the system's not working, and most people aren't happy. But being *shomer negiah* just isn't feasible in this society."

I had just finished reading an interesting and very disturbing book about traditional Chinese women.

"Imagine this," I wrote back. "You are traveling through China and come across a small village where life is essentially the same as it was a century ago. There you meet an illiterate 15-year-old girl. In a year, she'll be forced to marry a man whom her parents selected long ago and in whom she has no interest. She'll be expected to serve him like a slave. And that, basically, will be her life.

"She listens wide-eyed as you describe your world. You tell her that women in your society are fully educated and can pursue any field. They choose when and whom they'll marry, and aspire to a relationship based upon mutual respect and love.

" 'It all makes so much sense,' she says with a sigh. 'But over here, it's another world. I know the system is unjust, and I'm unlikely to end up happy. But getting an education and having the kind of marriage you describe just isn't feasible in this society.'

"I think you'd reply, 'Listen to me! We're talking about your life! If you can't get what you want here, then get out!' "

Tragically, such a young woman may find it practically impossible to pick up and leave, and even if she did, the social consequences might be unbearable. Unlike her, however, most of us have considerable freedom. The question is whether we exercise it. When "the system isn't working," we can "go with the flow" — or gravitate, at our own pace, toward a community of people leading more intelligent and rewarding lives. Like our great-

great-grandparents, we can assimilate into the surrounding culture — or dare to be different, with all the benefits of that difficult choice. It's up to us.

Where's the Romance?

Q. Doesn't a relationship feel cold and sterile if you can't get physical? Where's the romance?

"Romance" is one of those words that gets thrown around a lot while rarely being defined. In fact, it can mean a few things. There's what's known as classical romance; there's modern romance; and then there's what I call genuine romance. So before even attempting to answer the burning question, "Can David and Deborah be *shomer negiah* and still experience romance?", we have to clarify which kind we're talking about.

Let's look first at the classical variety and how it originated, which takes us back to the Middle Ages:

Take one Knight and one Fair Lady. Knight, like most males, has a distinct preference for beautiful women. The more religious side of his nature, however, dictates that it is noble to love only that which is good and pure (as opposed to that which is merely pleasing to the eye). To satisfy the demands of both his religion and his male psyche, Knight comes up with an ingenious strategy: He'll use his imagination to infuse physical beauty with virtue. Milky-white skin will translate into purity of the soul, majestic bearing into upright behavior, an elegant walk into inner grace, and so on, until he can idolize not only Fair Lady's looks but her spirit.

But now Knight is left with two knotty problems. First, physically expressing his passion for

Fair Lady will rid her of the very purity that justifies it. Second, his fantasy of Fair Lady's physical and spiritual perfection will be shattered if he ever gets close enough to see the pimples under her makeup.

The solution to both problems? "Love from afar." And thus classical romance is born. You might call it unacted-upon, religiously institutionalized infatuation — the key ingredient being a totally illusory view of one's beloved.

Traditionally, then, romance did not even involve physical closeness. However, since chastity and self-restraint no longer rank among the top ten virtues, "love from afar" has lost its appeal. Now, when two people cook up a relationship, they generally season it with a healthy measure of physical intimacy — hence the popular modern version of romance.

But modern romance is a complicated business, since being too close for too long eventually destroys all the mystery that provides fertile ground for illusion. The challenge, therefore, is to include just enough physical intimacy to fan the flames of passion without extinguishing them. Unfortunately, it's difficult to pull this off while still living your lives together. For you'll soon realize that your relationship stands a better chance of surviving if you restrict it to weekends or even once-a-month rendezvous. You'll also want to create the sensation of being in another world. Among the preferred activities are candlelit dinners (with physical imperfections fading into the shadows), walks on the beach, midnight strolls under starry skies, etc. Activities to be avoided include taking out the garbage, changing dirty diapers, mowing the lawn — in short, anything resembling reality. Modern romance may be great stuff for movies, but in real life, it doesn't work.

Stalwart defender of reality that it is, Judaism nonetheless recognizes that a small dose of illusion is very good for a relationship. The whole issue revolves around when illusion is introduced, and whether it includes physicality.

We've discussed the idea of maintaining objectivity in dating. Being in touch with reality is crucial when you're getting to know someone you might end up marrying. Your feet have to be firmly planted on the ground, not three feet above it, and your head must be in this world. Encouraging illusions would be foolish and dangerous. And if this realism precludes "romance," even without physicality, that's certainly better than marrying the wrong person based on a romantic fantasy.

So when can you get "romantic?" Once you're engaged. Of course, this romance won't include the physical side, but as we've seen, physical closeness isn't essential to romance anyway. In any case, once the two of you decide to spend the rest of your lives together, there's no longer any need to see each other so objectively. I'm not saying you should disregard one another's imperfections — after all, part of your job once you're married will be to help your partner grow into the best person he or she can become, and this task requires some awareness of his or her faults. But there's no longer any point in dwelling on them. This is who you have, and this is who you want. Now's the time to revel in the positive. Delight in what's beautiful about the person you've chosen to marry. Let yourself be starry-eyed. And by all means, stay that way once you're married (and then, of course, you can add the physical side as well). There's nothing unhealthy about feeling that your spouse (or spouse-to-be) is the most incredibly special human being on earth.

But as pleasurable as this kind of romance is with your lifelong partner or partner-to-be, there's something even better. Worlds better. And unlike both classical and modern romance, it's no fantasy. On the contrary, its very reality is what makes it so wonderful. It is, quite simply, the powerful awareness that the two of you have chosen to unite for life, based not upon rose-tinted illusions but upon having seen enough of the good (and even the not-so-good) in each other to understand and appreciate who one another really is. That's *genuine* romance. No feeling is more all-encompassing, more joyful — or more real. And while physical closeness is definitely one of the most wonderful ways to express it, it's not even necessary. This kind of connection stands on its own. Which shouldn't be surprising, because physical closeness never determined it to begin with.

Non-physical romance is a great way to focus on the most attractive aspects of the person to whom you're engaged. Physical romance is an even better way to focus on the most attractive aspects of the person to whom you're married. But best of all is when your desire for each other is fueled by genuine romance — the kind developed in the absence of physical closeness, the kind that's real.

Genuine romance is what Andy meant when he called being *shomer negiah* "the most powerful love potion." In the end, nothing beats reality.

CHAPTER NINE

Great Expectations

L et's assume you've recognized the wisdom of the Jewish approach to relationships, and you've put it into practice. Now you've met someone very special. Rose-colored glasses have stayed in their case, leaving your view of this person and your relationship more objective. And in the space created by the physical distance you've maintained, something genuine has taken root and blossomed. Now, looking at the one you're with and what has grown, you know you've found the right person. You're ready to embark upon life's greatest spiritual odyssey: marriage.

Like everyone, you will be entering into marriage with expectations, both conscious and unconscious. These expectations can make or break your marriage. Some will be rooted in your relationship with your parents and in their own relationship with each other. Others will stem from your ideas about marriage — culled from books, friends, the media, as well as your own thinking. But all will be influenced by the sense of reality, or lack of it, that you have allowed to pervade your relationship from the beginning.

Life is anything but a fairy tale. As someone I know once very bluntly put it, "Life is mundane." Now I happen to know that this man has a great marriage, a beautiful family, and a deeply rewarding occupation that leaves him time to pursue even more fulfilling Torah study. His comment wasn't coming from negativity. So what did he mean?

Much of life is neither new nor exciting in the conventional sense. While many of us accept the "mundanity" of our domestic responsibilities or even our jobs, we somehow think marriage must be different. Granted, a marriage shouldn't stagnate; it shouldn't be "the same old thing" year after year. For anything to remain alive, it must always be changing and growing. Yet there are different kinds of change and growth, and these create different kinds of newness and excitement.

When a baby is born, he or she changes visibly nearly every day. Parents (I can tell you) are constantly taking pictures, and long-distance grandparents (my mother can tell you) complain if they don't receive prints in the mail every couple of weeks. But as the child matures, change slows considerably. The difference between a 5-year-old and a 6-year-old is far subtler than that between a newborn and a 4-month- old.

So, too, with relationships. In the beginning, every day reveals new worlds about your partner — and about yourself. As time passes, however, the revelations grow fewer and smaller as you find yourself in increasingly familiar territory. Then the reality of marriage can loom large, but if you're prepared for it, you can welcome it. For though Judaism provides ways of periodically re-experiencing the thrill of being newlyweds, marriage ultimately has something far greater to offer. Much of the excitement you once knew should ideally be metamorphosing into a quieter, deeper kind: an excitement born not of newness, but of the sense that the two of you are slowly but surely merging into one.

To experience the joy of a lifelong relationship, you must be able to find excitement in nothing more than everyday life — utter reality. This ability will come naturally if your expectations of marriage have been nurtured in an atmosphere of reality, an atmosphere based on a realistic view of your partner and your relationship. And this, as we have seen, is what being *shomer negiah* has helped you create.

The Jewish world is built on happy marriages. While making things work after the wedding takes time and effort, Judaism gives us a way, while still dating, to greatly increase the likelihood of achieving that successful, lifelong union. Perhaps in the end, this realism is the essence of the Jewish approach to relationships.

CHAPTER TEN

"But We're Just Friends..."

W e've discussed the benefits of being *shomer negiah* in romantic relationships. But even if not touching makes sense when you're dating, how about when you aren't? What's wrong with a friendly touch, hug, or kiss between a guy and a girl who are "just friends"?

Here we enter the deep and murky waters of that phenomenon popularly known as "platonic relationships." There are several varieties, and none of them are simple. That's because God created men and women to be attracted to one another. So while you and your friend may not be doing anything physical, what you're likely to be feeling is another issue.

In the first kind of "platonic relationship" — the kind most people think they have — neither party has any romantic interest in each other. In truth, this utter absence of hormones is highly uncommon. If it weren't, the earth's population wouldn't be where it is. Furthermore, such relationships don't necessarily stay that way, for one day, either or both of you may find that other person growing on you. Then your relationship has graduated to something else.

The second variety is more complex: one of you is attracted, the other not. If you're the one feeling the attraction, you're undoubtedly keeping quiet — either because you're afraid of jeopardizing the relationship, or because you're a coward. At the same time (particularly if you're male), you're probably experiencing considerable physical frustration. I recall a very affectionate female acquaintance who would often bid her male friend good-bye with a big, long, warm hug. Finally he couldn't take it anymore. "You know," he told her, "when you give me one of those hugs, I'm feeling more than you realize, and it's not easy." ("Platonic relationships" are yet another area in which women conveniently forget how men work.)

If your attraction is of a deeper, romantic sort, you're suffering even more pain. When you're with your "buddy," you probably feel as if there's a knife in your gut. And whenever he or she says goodbye with a friendly kiss on the cheek (instead of the kiss you're dying for), the knife gets pushed farther in, until you're hemorrhaging inside.

Meanwhile, let's peek inside your "friend" 's mind. Though seemingly oblivious, he or she usually senses what's going on but chooses not to recognize it. For example, a woman I know was surprised to learn that a man with whom she had been friendly some years back had in fact had a crush on her. Upon reflection, however, she realized that part of her had always known, but she hadn't wanted to acknowledge it for fear of complicating the friendship.

Alternately, your friend may be fully aware of how you feel and (while still feigning innocence) be positively enjoying it. A woman will usually admit that it's downright fun to bask in the glow of a male friend's attraction. She may even confess to loving the power that comes from choosing not to respond. I suspect that a man with a secretly adoring female friend finds it similarly gratifying. Either way, someone's ego is being stroked at the expense of someone else's feelings.

Of course, the attraction may not remain one-sided. Which brings us to the third kind of "platonic relationship": You're both attracted, but for whatever reason (often because neither is sure what the other is feeling), no one's doing anything about it. In this case, it's just a matter of time before the truth comes out — and then it will be awfully hard to keep your kisses and hugs merely friendly. While self-control is a virtue, constantly testing that virtue is asking for trouble.

To sum up, any male-female relationship is only superficially "platonic"; beneath the surface, there's always more going on.

If you nevertheless seek a "platonic relationship" with someone attractive, you can try and switch off your more-than-friendly instincts. However, since sexual feelings between a man and a woman are about the most natural thing there is, pretending they don't exist isn't healthy. And on a societal level, if we all tell ourselves we're not feeling what we're feeling, the result is mass confusion about relationships.

It's very telling that "platonic relationships" gained popularity at the same time as another major cause of social confusion: "casual relationships." In a casual physical relationship, two people are doing the most intimate thing possible with their bodies with no corresponding emotional intimacy. If you're sensitive, you may feel there's something wrong with this. Yet you may not recognize a "platonic relationship" as simply the other side of the coin. Here, two people are achieving greater and greater emotional closeness without permitting it any physical expression. Both kinds of relationship are unnatural: Rather than working together as an organic unit, body and soul are out of sync.

Having a good friend of the opposite sex is especially problematic once you're married. If you're a newlywed, particularly if you're religious, you may have known your spouse for only a few months to a year. Even if you two have dated for a long time, marriage marks something new. No matter how deeply you know that your spouse is the right one and how much you feel for him or her, your bond is still embryonic. It takes a lot of work during that first challenging year to develop a viable relationship, and this job requires all your emotional attention. The last thing you need is for any of your energy to be diverted into an opposite-sex friendship — especially one that involves touch.

Maybe you know a couple like the following one. Naomi and Dan met the last year of medical school, got married after graduation, and began their internships. Spending most of her waking hours at work, Naomi soon became friendly with a resident named Larry. Whenever she'd have a disagreement with Dan, she'd tell Larry about it, and he would console her — and sometimes rub her back a little to make her feel better. After a while, she and Larry began going out together for coffee breaks to talk about things, and the once-in-a-while back rubs turned into frequent, warm hugs. Then they started having an occasional dinner together after their shifts were over. By this time Naomi was starting to feel closer to Larry than to Dan — and they were each sensing something more beneath their hugs. (I'll skip the end of the story. Let's just say that workplaces are notorious breeding grounds for unkosher relationships.)

Now rewind the movie, and imagine that Naomi and Larry, rather than having recently become acquainted, had been close friends for three years. Chances are the screen time will be significantly reduced.

True, a great many relationships of this sort do not culminate in an affair. Yet, to the Jewish mind, an intimate friendship with someone of the opposite sex compromises your marital bond. It could be called emotional infidelity.

Many people of marriageable age have serious male-female friendships. This is not — I repeat, *not* — a good way to start a marriage. If you doubt it, then ask yourself if you'd want the person you marry to have a good, longstanding friend of the opposite sex. And now ask yourself if you'd feel better or worse knowing that they regularly exchanged friendly back rubs and hugs. If such a threesome would not make you happy, then do your future spouse and marriage a favor, and figure out a sensitive way to cool down your own opposite-sex friendships.

From a Jewish viewpoint, a "platonic relationship" is like playing with matches — and expressing your affection through touch is like igniting the whole pack at once. Someone's going to get burned. If you're smart, you'll keep your relationships with the opposite sex low-key and "hands off." Save all that energy for the real thing.

CHAPTER ELEVEN

Showing You Care

Throughout this book, the focus has been on you — what *you* gain and what *you* avoid by being *shomer negiah*. But Judaism teaches us that responsibility cannot stop at our own doorstep. Every relationship involves two people, and each person's approach affects the other. So whether or not you feel you owe it to yourself to be *shomer negiah*, maybe you owe it to someone else.

An old friend of mine named Jodi had an experience that drove this point home to her. Traveling through Europe on her way to Israel, she met a young Italian Jew named Antonio. The two liked each other immediately and spent a few romantic days together. Jodi's affection for Antonio, however, wasn't enough to keep her in Italy while her Eurailpass expired. So she bade him goodbye, sure that their relationship would leave him with no more than fond memories.

But she was wrong. Three months later, in Jerusalem, she found a letter from Italy in her mailbox.

"I feel so sad and lonely ever since you left," Antonio wrote. "I think of you every waking moment, and each day I'm falling more and more in love with you."

At first, Jodi was flattered. But that feeling soon gave way to sorrow and dismay as she realized, "Oh, no — what have I done?"

To Jodi, their brief relationship had seemed harmless. Antonio had known she wouldn't be staying, and to make parting easier, she had held physical involvement with him to a minimum. Nonetheless she had unwittingly encouraged a full-fledged infatuation, and now she felt largely responsible for his unhappiness.

Antonio did get over her and is now married. But as Jodi became more sensitive to physical relationships, she realized that he could regain his happiness but never that measure of singularity he would otherwise have known with his wife. While Jodi knew she was not Antonio's only such romance, she deeply regretted her part in his loss.

Few of us may feel as strongly as Jodi. But perhaps we should. A person who knows how bad smoking is may lack the will power to quit, but he or she still may not want to give someone else a cigarette. Similarly, however much or little concern you feel for yourself, you're probably sensitive enough to feel for others. Rather than damaging them, you want to help them get the best out of life, which means — among other things — helping them actualize everything we've discussed. You want to help them develop an appreciation of reality that will increase their chances of entering into marriage with the right person and with realistic expectations. You want to spare them pain and disillusionment. And you want to enable them to enjoy as much specialness and genuine romance as possible with their soulmate.

When you reserve physical closeness for your ultimate relationship, you are doing much more than simply looking out for your own interests. Being *shomer negiah* says you care not only about yourself but about others.

CHAPTER TWELVE

Leading the Way

A depressing resignation pervades the dating scene today. If you're like many people I've met, you realize things don't often work out as you wish — yet you wonder sadly if anything can be done. Maybe you feel stuck, bound by social expectations, by "the way things are." Maybe you're also afraid of being lonely. So you get physically involved, which provides a temporary high yet rarely culminates in that ultimate relationship you're craving.

But could it be that you're underestimating people? Like you, other sensitive souls out there may very well be open to trying something different — if only someone would show them the way.

Believe it or not, the Talmud (*Menachot* 44a) recounts such a story.

There was once a young Jewish man who scrupulously observed the commandment of *tzitzit*. (*Tzitzit* is a mitzvah in which strings are attached to any four-cornered garment, reminding a Jew of his religious and moral obligations, particularly the injunction not to "stray after your eyes.") Despite this man's general piety, however, he had a major weak-

ness for women. One day he heard about a phe-
nomenally high-priced, gentile harlot who lived far
away. Deciding this was an experience he had to
have, he sent his messenger to arrange a date and
deliver full payment.

Months in advance, the man began his journey. When the long-awaited day and time arrived,
he was waiting at her door, and was shortly admit-
ted by a maidservant. The harlot then appeared in
all her breathtaking beauty. She presented her cli-
ent with a dazzling display: seven beds, each higher
than the last, the first six made of silver and connected by silver ladders, with the final ladder and
bed made of gold.

The harlot ascended all the ladders, lay down
on the golden bed, and waited for him. He scram-
bled up eagerly after her. But just as he reached the
top, something incredible happened: his *tzitzit* rose
up and smacked him in the face. Shaken, he beat a
hasty retreat back down.

The harlot had no idea what had caused this as-
tounding about-face — nothing like this had ever
happened to her. She too descended the ladders
and sat down with him.

"I swear by Rome," she said, "that you're not
leaving until you tell me what blemish of mine
drove you away."

"I swear by the Temple," he answered, "that
never in my life have I seen a woman as beautiful as
you. But there's a precept God has commanded us,
called *tzitzit*, and we're told that both its punish-
ment and its reward are very great. And my *tzitzit*
just struck my face like four witnesses testifying
against me."

The harlot was blown away. "Before you leave," she told him, "I want to know your name, where you're from, your rabbi, and where you study Torah."

He wrote it all down for her and departed.

The harlot sold off her entire estate. The only possession she kept were the sheets that had adorned the golden bed.

She traveled all the way to the man's city, located his place of study, and approached his teacher. "Rabbi," she said, "I want to convert to Judaism."

It wasn't every day that a gorgeous, gentile woman came to this scholar with a request to become Jewish. Skeptical about her sincerity, the rabbi asked, "Could it be that you've set your sights upon one of my students?"

In reply, she described the miracle of the *tzitzit* and how it had moved her to embrace Judaism.

Amazed, the rabbi agreed to the woman's conversion. "Now go and enjoy your prize," he said, giving her his blessing to marry his pupil.

In the happy ending, the very sheets on which the couple nearly sinned were used for their wedding night. And the Talmud concludes, "How great is the reward in this world for the mitzvah of *tzitzit* — and who knows how much greater in the world to come!"

My initial reaction to reading this story was "WHAT?! This is the Talmud talking — you know, that great compendium of profound Jewish thought. Am I to believe that this guy's 'great reward' for keeping the mitzvah of *tzitzit* was nothing loftier than getting to marry the world's most beautiful ex-prostitute?"

But after thinking about it, I realized that there was much more to this deeply moving tale and to the reward in question. Here was a woman living in a world dominated by lust, working in the most degrading business imaginable — and this man opened her eyes to spirituality. Furthermore, in the wake of that powerful experience, she left her entire life behind (including a lucrative career) in search of truth. How rewarding to play such a role in another person's life!

But that's not all. In the end, he was privileged to marry this woman of amazing inner strength and integrity. Apparently, her beauty was more than skin-deep.

This story, like all those recorded in the Talmud, remains as relevant as ever. And it contains a profound message of hope.

True, today a guy's *tzitzit* (if he's even wearing them) are unlikely to slap him in the face to prevent him from doing something wrong, thereby inspiring some beautiful woman to join him on life's journey (or vice versa). But this story is about something no less impressive than a miracle: the ability to resist temptation for the sake of something greater.

Imagine yourself on a date with a very attractive person. It's getting late, the energy between you is good, and it feels natural to take that exciting step into a physical relationship. But you stop a minute. You take a deep breath. And then you look into his or her eyes and say: "You know, you're the most beautiful woman/man I've ever met, and part of me would love to become physically involved with you right now. But there's a precept I adhere to

— it's called 'not selling either of us short.' While not getting physical may be difficult now, I believe it will pay off in the long run. So how about if we wait, get to know each other better, and see what there really could be between us."

If I were a typical non-religious woman, and a man said that to me, once I got over my shock, I'd be overwhelmed with awe and admiration. In fact, I'd probably fall at his feet. A man's response to such a speech might be less enthusiastic, but if he really likes you — and if he's worth anything — he'll rise to the challenge. If not, what have you lost? Move on and find someone who's interested in you for who you are.

But whether you're a man or a woman, you, too, just might spark someone else's spiritual awakening — and given the genuine relationship that may then develop, who knows how great your reward will be?

Afterword

Y ou know, a very interesting thing has been happening in secular society. Here and there, increasing numbers of sensitive individuals are quietly redefining their concept of "liberation." Back in the '60s and '70s, being "liberated" meant doing whatever you wanted with whomever you wanted without inhibition or guilt. People deluded themselves into thinking that physical relationships devoid of love, exclusivity, and commitment were the key to self-awareness, self-expression, and growth. Many folks still think this way. But they're wrong, and the tragic consequences of their error include an unprecedented divorce rate and untold desensitization to one of the most beautiful and rewarding aspects of life — not exactly what one would call "liberation."

Lately, however, amidst the clamor left in the wake of the sexual revolution, I've been hearing a new voice. This voice is defining liberation the opposite way — and asking others to wake up and do the same. It's the voice of those who don't want to sell anyone short, including themselves. A young, secular woman I'll call Lisa put it like this:

"Not long ago, I decided I'd had it with getting physical in a relationship just because that's what was expected. I felt I was giving in to social pressure at the expense of experiencing something more real and satisfying. It's taken a long time, but I've finally developed the belief in myself to say to someone, 'I'm not interested in getting involved physically right now, but if you'd really like to get to know me, I'd really like to get to know you.' "

So, too — almost — in more observant circles. In my discussions with young women (and occasionally men) from traditional homes, who have stopped somewhat short of being *shomer negiah*, I hear the same feelings being expressed, but more falteringly. Someone — let's call her Leah — will ask to speak to me privately after a class on Jewish dating. Once she's sure no one is listening, she'll confess, "I agree with everything you say. I know most of my friends would, too. It all makes so much sense. It's just that no one else I know is actually doing it. I don't know if I'm strong enough to be the first. Maybe if a group of us all started together...."

Why is it easier for the Lisas to take a stand than for the Leahs?

First of all, Lisa is usually older — at least in her mid-twenties — and has gotten where she is the hard way. Often "burnt out," she has seen and done enough to know very clearly what she wants and doesn't want, and why. Leah is generally younger and less experienced, and for her, the prospect of physical closeness in dating hasn't yet lost its allure.

Second, because Lisa has moved beyond the overwhelming adolescent and post-adolescent need for social approval (and in any case, her previous behavior has already earned her the dubious title of "normal"), she's in a better position to deal with flak about her decision. In contrast, because Leah still seeks peer acceptance, she often lacks the self-confidence to act independently.

Finally, there's the image factor. The Lisas I know, who are reclaiming their "right to self-determination" in relationships, are seen as flag-bearers of a new consciousness. You can get away with almost anything perceived as "new," "progressive," or even "radical." Then, even if people disagree with it, you're cool. "Ancient," on the other hand, doesn't have the same ring in today's superficial, image-oriented society. For Leah, returning to the beliefs of a 3000-year-old religion takes guts.

Yet if Leah can find the courage, she can spare herself everything Lisa had to go through to arrive at the same point.

Yes, our tradition is "ancient." But therein lies its power. Despite cultural upheavals, human psychology hasn't changed in three thousand years. And it never will. We will always need to love and be loved, to forge a lifelong spiritual and sexual union with one special person. We will always crave depth and realness and wholeness in that union. And we will always tend to bow to social pressure and miss the boat.

With all the complexities of relationships, it can be hard to know which road to take. But we have a signpost: In an act of overwhelming love, God gave us a piece of His infinite wisdom — the Torah — to help us find our way. For the problems surrounding relationships today are not new — and neither are the solutions. If Lisa can be considered a revolutionary, it's only because, God willing, we are finally coming full circle, where progressive and ancient meet.

About the Author

Gila Manolson (née Marilyn Fisch) grew up in the northeastern United States and graduated magna cum laude from Yale University with a degree in music. She later studied at Neve Yerushalayim College for Women, married, and settled in Jerusalem. For five years she was the resident supervisor of the women's branch of the Heritage House, a Jewish youth hostel in the Old City. She has taught in numerous programs and is a popular lecturer in Israel and abroad. She is also the author of *Outside/Inside: A Fresh Look at Tzniut* and *Head to Heart: What to Know Before Dating and Marriage*. She and her husband, Avraham, have seven children.